Maui
SNARES
the SUN

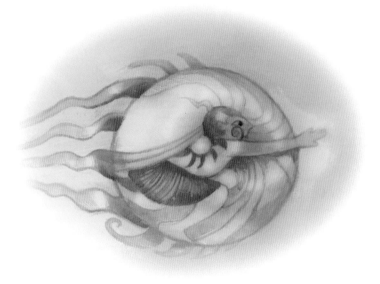

A traditional story retold by
Kate Keenan
Art by Pamela Becker

Literacy Consultants
David Booth • Kathleen Corrigan

Contents

CHAPTER 1

How the Sun and Moon Came to Be

Not enough time in the day? Tamaka, if you only knew! When I was a boy, the days were so much shorter than they are now.

No, don't pull your fishing nets in yet. You must give the fish a chance to swim inside first. Patience, my grandson. The sun won't set for hours. Here, sit down. Have some coconut water, and let the boat do the work for a while. I will tell you the story of when there truly was not enough time in the day.

Where should I begin? Well, there was once a time when the sun sped through the sky, so the days were short and the nights were long. Who knows why this was? There are some from the Kingdom of Tonga who tell the tale of Vatea, the father of all people, who had a quarrel with Tonga-iti over the firstborn child of the earth mother, Papa.

Tonga-iti and Vatea were both very stubborn gods, and both wanted to possess the child. After much arguing, two children were created from the one, and each god took a child for his own.

This solution did not end their quarrel, however.
To show he was more powerful than Tonga-iti, Vatea
rolled his child into a ball and threw him up into the
sky, where he glowed with a brightness like nothing
ever seen before. Tonga-iti was so amazed by this that
he dropped his child to the ground as he watched the
brilliant ball of fire travel across the sky. Can you guess
what this became? That's right — it became the sun!

Tonga-iti was very jealous of Vatea's magnificent creation. He picked up his child, who lay cold and pale on the ground. Tonga-iti threw the child up into the sky anyway and it became — what do you think? The moon of course! But so weak she was that she crawled across the sky as slowly as a snail.

Vatea had given the sun such a strong throw that it raced across the sky, making the days much shorter than these nice long summer days we have now. Can you imagine a world like that? Well, grandson, that is the world into which I was born.

CHAPTER 2

The Birth of Maui-tikitiki-a-Taranga

Yes, your grandfather, the great Maui-tikitiki-a-Taranga, was a baby once too! I've not always been the wise, old man you see before you. I began as a baby like you and so many others, but I was so small that my mother didn't think she could care for me. She wrapped me up in her *tikitiki* — the topknot of her hair — and sent me out to sea in the hope that the gods would save me.

The waves washed over me and seaweed tangled around my tiny body, but the Wind Folk blew me to the edge of the sea where my own grandfather,

Tamanui-ki-te-rangi, the Son of the Sky, scooped me up and saved me. Your grandfather may be a great man indeed, but my grandfather is a god!

My grandfather raised me and taught me many things, including the ways of the woodland animals — especially the birds. See that albatross following our boat?

Caw! Caw!

Watch it dive down into the waves, returning with — guess what? Yes, a nice fresh squid right in your lap.

Thank you, old albatross!

Did you know I could speak to the birds? One day I'll have to teach you this lesson.

When I turned eighteen, I told my grandfather that I wanted to find my mother. After traveling very far to reach her, I finally arrived at her hut. It was nighttime, so I decided to slip in the door and hide behind the swirling smoke of the fire that warmed the hut. I heard my mother call out to my four brothers.

"Maui-taha, Maui-roto, Maui-pae, Maui-waho, come to dinner!"

"You have forgotten one son!" I called from behind the smoke.

"I called you all! Which of you four boys is tricking your own mother?" scolded Taranga.

"It is your fifth son, Maui-tikitiki!" I shouted as I let myself be seen.

At first she didn't believe me, but when I called her by her name and told her of my adventures after she put me out to sea in her tikitiki, she wrapped me up in her arms.

"My own tiny Maui-tikitiki, I knew you would find a way! Boys, come and meet your brother!"

But my brothers were never fond of me, and I can't say I blame them! Right from that first trick with the smoke, I never stopped playing pranks on them. When we flew kites, mine would dart in the wind, like a petrel bird, tangling their lines. When we threw darts, I could make mine go the farthest of all. I could dive as deep as a booby bird, always snatching up the best oysters. And when my brothers got angry and chased me, I could turn myself into a bird and would fly up into the trees! Oh, I was full of mischief in those days!

What is that look? Ha, you're right! I'm still full of mischief! Now where was I? Oh, right, the short days of the old days!

CHAPTER 3

When Days Were Too Short to Do Anything

Can you imagine it, Tamaka? Only a few hours of sunlight a day. No wonder my brothers couldn't take a joke — they were so frustrated! Every day they would just manage to paddle their boats out to sea and cast their nets when the sun would start to set, and then they'd have to head back to shore!

"What is your hurry, Sun? Please slow down so that we can pull in a good catch and feed our families!" They would call this out to the sun, but the sun was full of pride and wouldn't listen to the pleas of the humans way down on Earth. Onward it sped so that it could sleep all the long night.

It wasn't only my brothers who could not get work done either. My own mother, Taranga, could not make her *kākahu*! Tamaka, you have seen how your great-grandmother makes your and everyone's clothes, yes?

She uses fibers called *muka* from the *harakeke* tree. I'm sure you're wondering how it is possible to wear strips of leaves. Well, your grandmother first scrapes the muka with a mussel shell, then rolls it and soaks it and beats it, and finally, she rubs it by hand to make it soft enough to weave. (It is not easy work — this is why your great-grandmother has strong muscles.) After all that work, your great-grandmother would set the muka out in the sun to dry. But in those days, no sooner had she laid it out to dry than that lazy sun would rush off to bed, and she'd have to gather up all the muka and start again the next day!

On one long, dark night, we sat in our hut, listening to our stomachs rumbling with hunger, wet muka hung everywhere, and I decided I'd had enough! If that sun would not listen to the people, I would make him listen! I was determined.

My brothers all laughed at me, but my mother understood the unwavering look in my eyes. "If you are truly set on this quest, son, go and seek your grandmother, Muriranga-whenua. She prepares the sun his breakfast of fried bananas every morning. She does not know you, but if you can win her favor, she will help you."

I set off that very moment, traveling through the long night so that the sun would not suspect my plan. The journey was long and tiring, but I had set my body and mind to the task. As I walked and walked, I thought of different scenarios — and their consequences — and before I knew it, I had reached the great volcano where Muri lived. I climbed and climbed in the darkness until I reached the dormant crater at the summit. It was so lush with vegetation — it was hard to imagine that just below the ground boiled fiery lava!

I crept through the trees until I finally caught sight of my grandmother Muri gathering bananas. Now, Tamaka, you think your great-grandmother Taranga is fierce? Muri was like Taranga, but with the tail of a scorpion! She had lost her sight completely, but her sense of smell was stronger than ever — she could smell someone coming from a mile away!

I crept over to her from the north and snatched a bunch of bananas. She sniffed the air suspiciously, but I rubbed my skin with a banana skin and circled around to the south, grabbing another bunch of bananas. She swiveled around and shouted, "Who dares to steal from Muri? Show yourself, thief!"

She sniffed where I had been, but by then I was coming in from the east for a third bunch of bananas. Again she turned and sniffed, crying, "When I catch you, trickster, you'll be in big trouble!"

I crept in from the west, but the wind was blowing from that direction, and she sniffed me through my banana scent. She lunged forward to snatch me, but her gnarled hands clutched the giant pile of bananas I had left in my place. I put my arms around her from behind.

"Would you really not recognize your own grandson?" I laughed.

She turned and felt my face. "You are lucky you are so clever. I believe you since only a grandson of mine could have tricked me like that! Now, what do you want? Speak your mind!"

I laughed again and said, "I've come to confront the great sun whose breakfast you prepare every morning."

"That sun will listen to no man!"

"He will if you help me."

"So that's the only reason that you have come to visit your grandmother."

"And to steal your bananas!"

"You are a trickster indeed," Muri laughed. "You may be a match for the sun after all. What you must do is ensnare him, but any rope you make from flax will burn to a crisp in his fiery rays. You must weave a rope from the hair of your own sister, Hina."

"Thank you, grandmother," I said, kissing her on the cheek as I turned to leave.

"Wait," Muri said, pulling me back. "Take this, my grandson. It will help you for the rest of your life."

Then what do you think she did? She offered me a piece of her jawbone! She placed it in my hand and for the first time in my life, I could think of nothing to say. Muri laughed again, mumbled something I couldn't understand, and then shooed me away.

I left Muri's volcano and journeyed to the sea in search of my sister. When I finally reached the sea, I became a booby bird so that I could dive deep down to visit my sister, Hina. I found her in her underwater garden, teaching tricks to her sea horses.

I turned myself back into a man, and when she saw me, she scowled.

"Is that how you greet a brother you have never met?" I asked.

"Tales of your mischief come down on the ocean currents. I know that if you are here, it is because you want something from me," she answered, crossing her arms. Her long silver hair floated all around her as she spoke, and I knew she would never give me any if I asked — even if I asked nicely.

"I've come for nothing," said I, with a wounded air. "In fact, I come with a present for my noble sister, Lady of the Fish."

Out of my own hair, I pulled an intricately carved bone comb. My sister reached out for the beautiful object — a look of distrust in her eyes.

"Allow me the honor of combing your hair for you," I said.

As I ran the comb through her hair, strand upon strand of silver hair floated away. You see, I had sharpened the teeth of the comb so that it cut through her delicate hair like a knife. I caught the floating strands between my fingers and hid them away in my sack. My sister had so much hair that she didn't notice I had taken some. She thanked me for the comb, and I swam back up to the surface.

I wonder how long it took her to comb all of her hair right off and discover my trick. There must have been a storm at sea that night, ha-ha!

CHAPTER 4

Snaring the Sun

When I returned to my family's hut, we all set to making rope — thick, twisted, square, and flat rope, each one stronger than the last. Intertwined were the silver strands of Hina's hair. We coiled the rope into giant bundles, and my brothers and I hauled them on our backs and headed east. We walked many nights until we came to the giant chasm where the sun lays his fiery head to sleep.

We built huge barriers consisting of clay to shield ourselves from the sun's ferocious rays. Then we created a vast network of snares with the ropes and slung them across the chasm. We crouched behind our shelters and waited for the sun to rise.

I could tell my brothers seemed reluctant to continue our quest.

"Maybe short days aren't so bad," said Maui-waho.

"They have to be better than charred cinders — which is what we're about to become!" said Maui-pae.

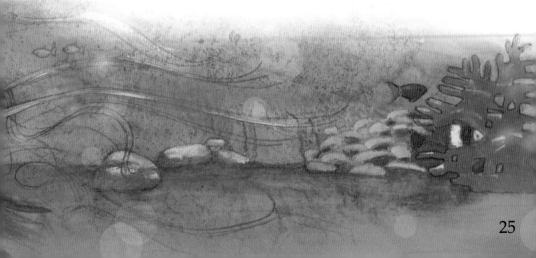

At that moment, we heard the roar of a hundred typhoons and felt the heat of a hundred wildfires. Out of the chasm blazed a light so bright that it blinded us! Our clay shelters exploded into white ash, and it felt as if our flesh were melting off our bodies.

For a moment, I thought my brothers were right and this would be the end of us, but then I felt something moving in my sack. I opened it and saw Muri's jawbone — quivering and glowing white. I pulled it out and held it in the air. Suddenly a cool shadow fell over us, protecting us from the sun's burning heat.

Just then, one of the sun's rays inched its way out of the chasm.

"Now!" I yelled, and Maui-taha pulled the first snare tight. The ray pulsated and jerked, but it was caught fast. Then more rays slithered out of the hole.

"Now, now, now!" And we hauled on our snares with all the strength we could muster.

Then, the giant fireball itself shot out of the chasm, screaming in rage. It thrashed like a hooked barracuda, but it was no use: the sun was caught!

"Release me!" the sun howled.

I tried to yell back, but the noise was so great that I couldn't hear my own voice. Just then, the jawbone started to quiver again. I brought it to my mouth. I called through it, and now my voice boomed over the din, suddenly giving me a sense of power.

"Stop your struggling and listen to me, Sun!"

"Who dares address the great Tama-nui-te-rā?" roared the sun.

And that is how we came to learn the sun's true name — Great Son of the Sun.

CHAPTER 5

A Compromise

"It is the people of Earth, Tama-nui-te-rā! We ask that you slow your path in the sky! You speed so quickly that we have no time to finish our work."

"I am the strongest, most powerful being in all the heavens! Why should I listen to a puny human?"

"Because strong, powerful sun, this puny human has you caught!"

The sun screamed and thrashed in fury, but the jawbone began to glow, and its beam seemed to sap all the sun's strength. Tama-nui-te-rā sank down in defeat. This was a strange sight indeed.

"I offer you this compromise," he said. "In the summer I shall move slowly through the sky, and you will have plenty of time to get your work done. But in the winter I will rush back to my home, and the days will be as short as they are now."

I knew that the sun was indeed a great creature and no good would come of stealing all his pride.

"Release the snares!" I yelled to my brothers, and the sun shot up into the sky as the ropes fell away.

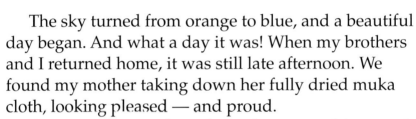

The sky turned from orange to blue, and a beautiful day began. And what a day it was! When my brothers and I returned home, it was still late afternoon. We found my mother taking down her fully dried muka cloth, looking pleased — and proud.

"It seems that you boys have done something good with your day."

"So have you, Mother!" I laughed.

And we all enjoyed many months of long summer days — as leisurely and lovely as this one today!

Now Tamaka, go and check the nets. I'm sure they are heavy with fish by now, and we shall have time to paddle home and cook a delicious dinner before the sun sets.